Heaven

Don Baker is pastor of First Evangelical Free Church in Rockford, Illinois. His books include *Depression, Pain's Hidden Purpose, Beyond Forgiveness, Beyond Rejection, Beyond Choices, Acceptance,* and *A Fresh New Look at God.*

Unless otherwise noted, all Scripture references are from the *Holy Bible: New International Version,* copyright 1973, 1978 by the International Bible Society. Used by permission of Zondervan Bible Publishers.

Scripture references marked NASB are from the New American Standard Bible, © The Lockman Foundation 1960, 1962, 1963, 1968, 1971, 1972, 1973, 1975, 1977.

Design by Michael S. Brown
Photography by Kris Coppieters—Belgium, Åke Lundberg

HEAVEN: A Glimpse of Your Future Home
© 1983 by Multnomah Press
Portland, Oregon 97266

Printed in Singapore

ISBN 0-88070-168-4

87 88 89 90 91 – 11 10 9 8 7 6 5 4 3 2

Don Baker

Heaven

MULTNOMAH · PRESS

Portland, Oregon 97266

Heaven

It was 2:10 in the morning. My brother Abe and I stood in opposite corners of a small, sterile hospital room, silent guardians of a precious life that was about to end. The only sound was our father's labored breathing as he struggled with the cancer that was killing him.

I moved to his bedside, laid my head wearily on his once strong arm, and waited. Occasionally I would speak: "Dad, Dad—it's Don—can you hear me?" There was no response, no flicker of the eyes, no movement of the lips—just silence.

His ragged breathing became even more difficult, the lapses between breaths further apart. And then—just for a brief moment—he raised both arms from the bed, held them there momentarily, and then let them fall. His final act of life.

Dad was dead. We had seen it coming for nearly three years. The cancer had invaded his body and then reached its pervasive fingers into every corner of his flesh.

Dad's death was not a surprise—but it was a shock. No matter how much forewarning we are given, death never ceases to be a shock.

For months prior to his death we had read John 14 to him. "In my Father's house are many mansions . . . I go to prepare a place for you. I will come again and receive you unto myself; that where I am, there ye may be also."

Whenever I'd ask what he'd like me to read, it was always the same. "John 14, son, John 14."

Just before he lapsed into a coma he took my mother in his arms and said, "Helen, the next time I see you, we'll be in our heavenly home."

As he spoke we were certain that we had heard our father's last words—and they were cherished words.

On the fourth day, however, he awakened with a somewhat startled expression on his face, and for just a few brief moments was lucid. He took my mother again in his arms and said, "Here we are, Helen, in our heavenly home." He then slipped back into the silent world of the dying and said no more.

Many times, as we have sat beside his graveside, pulling at the shaggy blades of grass and brushing clean his gravemarker, we have asked ourselves, "I wonder what it was that Dad saw in those moments as his spirit wavered between earth and Heaven."

Many have had similar experiences.

Before the advent of life-support systems and stupefying drugs, many were ushered from this life with a dignity that enabled them to die with awareness—and even to give partial descriptions of the experience.

Stephen, the church's first martyr, saw something as he was dying. As he gazed intently into Heaven, he saw the glory of God, and Jesus standing at the right hand of the Father.[1]

When the apostle Paul lay dying in the streets of Lystra[2] he saw things that no human could describe.[3]

There has been a growing fascination in recent years with death and dying experiences. Over a million copies of Dr. Raymond Moody Jr.'s book, *Life after Death,* and Dr. Maurice Rawlings's, *Beyond Death's Door,* have been purchased by a curious public who want to know what happens beyond the grave.

The place to go to find out about Heaven, however, is not the public library, nor the secular author, nor even the dying, but rather to Heaven's Creator and Number-One Tenant—God. We need to listen to Him as He gives us some fleeting verbal insights into the Scriptures.

Our Problem

When the apostle Paul uses the phrase "inexpressible words"[4] in reference to his "out-of-body" experience, he is defining our greatest problem in understanding Heaven.

Heaven is not limited to space and time. It's another dimension—beyond human comprehension. It's infinite, and infinite can never be understood by the finite.

That's why the Apostle Paul has told us that man's eyes, ears, and heart are unable to comprehend all that God has prepared for those who love Him.[5]

But let's try, anyway.

Its Location

Heaven is up. No matter what part of the globe I stand on, it's up. Now we knew that, didn't we? Yet in case you have fallen for the line of—

> the atheist, who claims that Heaven is the illusion of a spiritually intoxicated people,

> or the scientist, who claims that Heaven is nothing but a medieval fancy,

> or the liberal theologian, who views Heaven as a worn-out superstition,

> or the philosopher, who states that the Christian idea of Heaven is appallingly idiotic,

> or the Eastern mystic, who states that Heaven is the absence of existence—

then you need to be reminded that it's real and it's up.

Paul reminded us that when Jesus came to earth, He *descended,* and when He left earth, He *ascended.*[6]

The angels told the early disciples that Jesus had been taken *up* from them into Heaven.[7]

When the Lord comes, He will come *down,*[8] and when the church meets the Lord, it will be caught *up.*[9]

When God contemplates His creatures, He looks *down,*[10] and when man contemplates his God, he looks *up.*[11]

When John was about to be given a tour of Heaven, he was invited to "come *up.*"[12]

When the New Jerusalem is ready for occupancy, it will come *down.*[13]

Heaven is up—up, above the atmosphere, the troposphere, the stratosphere, the mesosphere, the ionosphere, and the exosphere. Up and beyond the Van Allen radiation belt and beyond interplanetary space.

Heaven is up—up and above our solar system, beyond our galaxy, beyond the thousand million galaxies in our universe, up and beyond 150 million million million stars, of which only 2,000 can be seen by the naked eye on a clear night.

Its Size

Heaven is up and is so big that at that incomprehensible distance it encircles not only our world, our solar system, our galaxy, but our universe as well.

It needs to be that big because that's how big our God is, and the Bible tells us that our God fills both Heaven and earth.[14]

Its Reality

Heaven is not a planet as we know a planet. It includes a planet and possibly many planets. The New Jerusalem has all the properties of a self-contained planet and is of immense size.[15]

Heaven is a place on the map of God. It's beyond the regions of all fancy. It's within the realm of the actual, the local. It's not made of air. It doesn't float around in some ethereal dream world. It's not a Disneyland. It's real and in contrast with earth, it's stable, secure, permanent, and eternal.[16] It has possibly many great cities,[17] and at least one of them, which is measurable and tangible,[18] has been prepared for us as our very own residence.[19]

What It's Like

Heaven contains many dwelling places.[20] John, in Revelation, visits God's residence first.[21] Using only the inadequate and antiquated language of earth, he describes a throne standing at the epicenter of the expanseless Heaven, on which was seated the measureless God. God's appearance was dazzling—like a magnificent multi-colored display of brilliant jewels.[22] The throne was bathed in the brilliance of a resplendent rainbow.[23]

Twenty-four other thrones stretched out beyond the central throne,[24] containing all of redeemed humanity's representatives—the elders in magnificent white robes with crowns of gold upon their heads.[25]

Heaven's majesty and wonder are accentuated with the periodic peals of thunder and flashes of lightning that originate from within the throne.[26]

The Holy Spirit is there in His perfect fullness, represented by seven great lamps of fire.[27]

The angelic beings are there, representing all of living creation.[28]

Jesus is there, and when He first appears to John in Heaven, since the redemptive program is not yet complete, He appears as a Lamb that was slain.[29]

The sound of music, music without discord, accompanied by magnificent harps,[30] reverberates in true high fidelity across Heaven. The elders and the angelic beings are joined by many angels and ultimately by every living creature in Heaven and on earth,[31] singing, "Worthy is the Lamb that was slain to receive power and riches and wisdom and might and honor and glory and blessing."[32]

As God fills Heaven and earth, so will this celestial music.

For one who loves music and gets goose bumps when the Hallelujah Chorus is sung, I cannot begin to imagine the effect of this magnificent choral number when it finally begins to waft out over the entire universe.

But for all of the compelling majesty and beauty of God's residence, that is not where we will be spending most of our time. I'm sure we'll all be taking periodic trips to this special place, but ours will be a different residence.

Heaven's High-Rise

John describes our house as a city—a place for corporate living, a city with walls and gates and streets and rivers, with buildings and people. A city without flaw, whose architect and builder was God.[33]

John uses a metaphor of consummate tenderness when he describes its radiant beauty as "a bride adorned for her husband."[34]

He describes its origin when he says it came down out of heaven from God.[35]

He describes its character when he calls it the Holy City.[36]

He describes its residents when he says it's the Tabernacle of God and the redeemed of all ages.[37]

He describes its splendor as that of having the glory of God and its brilliance as that of a dazzling, priceless jewel.[38]

He describes its immense size as 1500 miles wide and 1500 miles long or 2,250,000 square miles at the base and 1500 miles or 780,000 stories high—enough room to comfortably accommodate a hundred thousand million people—more than all the people who have ever lived.[39]

It has some unique and engaging features:

Magnificent, lasting tributes to the twelve tribes of the sons of Israel and to the twelve apostles of our Lord.[40]

For those who may be wondering whether or not we will remember what happened on earth and in life, it's interesting to note that God has already included some memorials in the eternal city.

The city has its own indirect lighting system, which requires no solar energy, nuclear energy, or hydroelectric power. The resplendent glory of both God the Father and God the Son shall illumine our city and not it only but also the entire new earth.[41] The sun and the moon as we know them today will be extinct.[42]

There will be no darkness.[43]

There will be no evil.[44]

There will be no famine and no drought since the city contains its own adequate water[45] and food supply.[46]

It's especially interesting to us earthbound people that our place in Heaven's High-Rise is already prepared,[47] and since it's part of our inheritance[48] it comes at no cost to us. This means

No down payment
No realtor fees
No closing costs
No mortgage payments
No property tax
No utility bills
No sewer assessments and
No fear of foreclosure.

I'm not sure whether our place is going to be a single-family residence, a condominium, a town house, an apartment, or something altogether different. I am certain, however, that it will be something far superior to anything anyone has ever known here on earth, and all this without maintenance, or upkeep.

Its view in all directions promises to be breathtaking.

Its glittering gold-paved streets, polished to appear like transparent glass, will be magnificent.[49]

Since there will be no pain in heaven, there will be no hospitals.

Since there will be no death, there will be no cemeteries.

Since there will be no tears, there will be no sorrow.

And since there will be no sin, there will be no regret.[50]

One other thing will be missing. No church building or temple will be there. In their place will be both the Father and the Son. All spiritual activity will revolve around the Persons rather than a structure.[51]

Its Occupants

It has been said that there will be three surprises in Heaven. We will be surprised—

to find some we did not expect,
to not find some we did expect, and
to find ourselves in Heaven.

I have always been fascinated with Heaven. When I was younger, though, I thought of Heaven only as a great shining city with vast walls and magnificent domes and soaring spires and with nobody in it but white-robed angels who were total strangers to me.

Then my beloved pastor died
and my grandfather died
and my father died
and my son died
and my father-in-law died
and then one-by-one, my dear friends
    began dying—three of them this
    past week.

Heaven is no longer walls and domes and spires, but people. People who are loved and missed—people who are precious and whose faces I long to see.

Heaven is like home in many respects. It's not *what* we have in our house that makes it precious, but *whom*.

Carefully consider Heaven's populace and it becomes increasingly precious. When you list the redeemed of all ages and add to that your own special list of loved ones and then add to that the presence of our Father and our Savior and our blessed Holy Spirit, Heaven becomes irresistible.

It's no wonder that God spared us a detailed description. Anymore and we would have been unwilling to wait. The Apostle Paul had only a fleeting glimpse, but what he saw was enough to make him spend the rest of his life on the tiptoe of expectancy, barely able to wait his turn.[52]

The society of Heaven will be select. There are many kinds of aristocracy in this world, but the aristocracy of Heaven will be one of holiness. The humblest sinner who repents will be an aristocrat there.

The humblest sinner who, while in this life, trusts in Jesus Christ will be an exalted member of the Heavenly Family there.

The Eternal City is for those who have made reservations here, for those who have trusted in Jesus Christ, God's Son.[53] Heaven is a prepared place for a prepared people, and preparation is made in the here and now of everyday life.

The city has not one gate but many. There are three gates on the north and three on the south and three on the east and three on the west,[54] and its peoples will come from all directions. From opposite quarters of the theological compass, from opposite quarters of human life and character, through different expressions of their common faith and hope, through different modes of conversion, and through different portions of Scripture will the weary travelers enter the Heavenly City, gathering as one on the shores of the river of life.

When we begin thinking about the inhabitants of heaven, it's right here that some of our most intriguing questions begin to surface.

Will We Know Each Other in Heaven?

Certainly! If anything we'll know each other better. Now our knowledge is limited—we know only in part; but there shall we know even as we are known.[55]

Jesus promised that in Heaven many shall come from all directions and sit down to eat with Abraham and Isaac and Jacob.[56]

On the Mount of Transfiguration, Peter, James, and John immediately recognized Moses and Elijah, though both had lived more than 900 years before.[57]

In each of these instances there is no hint of the need for an introduction.

It is interesting to note, however, that Jesus in His resurrected body was not immediately recognized on three separate occasions. This happened with Mary Magdalene,[58] the Emmaus disciples,[59] and with the twelve.[60] In each case He was not recognized until He spoke or acted, which seems to indicate a reversal of our present manner of knowing people. We now recognize people by how they look—their outward appearance; but then the recognition will be of what they are—we'll see beyond the externals into the true character of the person.

What Will We Look Like?

Better! I'm sure of it. We won't be disembodied spirits. We won't be angelic creatures with wings. We will lose our gender since we will be neither male nor female, just children—children of God.[61]

Since our bodies will be raised to house our spirits, there will probably be some resemblance to our past life. Jesus was able to prove the reality of His resurrection by His crucifixion scars.[62]

And yet we will be different.[63] Since our resurrected body will be designed for a new dimension, it will not be limited by space and time, and, like Jesus' body, will pass through matter[64] and probably move through space with the speed of thought.

Will We Be Married In Heaven?

No, we'll all be Career Singles. Since there is neither gender nor sex, there will be no marriage.

Our earthly relationships are very precious. We'd like to believe that they will continue forever. They cannot. Since the physical body as we now know it will no longer exist, physical relationships as we now know them will not be possible or necessary.

Earthly husband and wife will not be husband and wife in Heaven; parent and child will not be parent and child in Heaven.

If we feel a tinge of regret, don't be surprised; this is normal when we deeply love on earth. The closest relationships on earth will perhaps become a sweet memory in Heaven, but will be totally eclipsed by the glory of a new relationship there.

How Old Will We Be?

Since there is no time in eternity, there is no age. Some like to think of Jesus' age of thirty-three as the ideal age, but there is no indication of this in Scripture. Age implies aging, and that is something we will never do in Heaven.[65]

Do We Go To Heaven Immediately At Death?

Yes and No. The spirit, when separated from the body, is immediately at home with the Lord.[66]

For the spirit, made alive by Christ, there is no intermediate state, no purgatory, no limbo, no soul-sleep. This was the promise Jesus made to the dying thief on the cross.[67] This was the experience of our Lord, Himself, when He committed His spirit to God.[68]

The body, when separated from the spirit, remains behind temporarily. It may be buried, cremated, or lost, never to be found. That body, however, created by God and redeemed by Christ, is always of great value in Heaven, of such value that plans have been made to resurrect it.

When the Lord descends from Heaven, when the archangel shouts and when the trumpet of God blows, the graves are going to split asunder, the disintegrated molecules are going to re-form, and a body, made new and changeless, is going to appear. That new body will be caught up to be reunited with spirit, with Christ, and with the redeemed of all ages.[69]

Will We Be
Able to See What's
Happening on Earth?

The Scriptures say very little about this question. Samuel, after death, knew what was happening on earth.[70] Moses and Elijah, when they met Jesus on the mountain were conversant about what was happening on earth.[71] John, in Revelation, saw the souls of martyred saints in Heaven,[72] and the rich man from his place of torment in hell saw Lazarus in Paradise.[73]

Jesus sees us, and I would assume that if we have expanded knowledge and limitless capacity to move about the vastness of Heaven that we too shall be able to see what's happening here. But my questions is this: *Who would want to?*

If you've seen one earth, you've seen them all.

It took only one glimpse of Heaven for Paul to

say, I have a desire to depart and be with Christ, which is far better.[74]

Astronauts, as they orbit throughout space, spend little time studying earth. They are consumed by the new and the different and the unexplored.

I would imagine Heaven will consume most of our thought and most of our attention, for all that we shall see will be new and different and beyond any human imaginings in this life.[75] Earth will be part of the past, Satan's hovel, with little or no attraction for us. There are places and events in this life we'd like to forget, and I'm sure the same will be true of earth when we get to Heaven. We'll be so absorbed with the new, we'll not want to look at the old.

What Will We Do in Heaven?

The thoughts of sexless cherubs playing harps on fluffy clouds really doesn't move most of us. To spend eternity without meaningful activity, engaged only in one endless afternoon nap, doesn't excite us either.

Even to spend it all in performing as a member of the Heavenly Oratorio Society leaves most of us cold.

Actually, in Heaven we are going to do some of the same things we do here on earth, like

worship
  serve
    administer
      fellowship
        learn and
          rest.

The only difference is that it will be

    worship without distraction
      service without exhaustion
        administration without failure
          fellowship without suspicion
        learning without
        weariness and
          resting without
          boredom.

Worship will no longer be an indefinable word or an indescribable experience. It will not be manipulated or contrived. All its pretense lost, worship will be one of the first great and continuous activities for the redeemed.

It will be spontaneous and genuine. It will encompass the whole universe. The *hallelujahs* and the *praise the Lords* and the *amens* will drown out all of the sounds of Heaven and earth, and we will all lose ourselves in the joy of telling our God how much we adore Him.[76]

Service

We shall serve Him.[77] How or where I'm not sure. But the word "serve" is prominent in Revelation. On eight different occasions it describes our function in Heaven.

It will be service without time demands. Service without frustration. Service without fear of failure. Service without limitations. Service without exhaustion.

It may quite possibly be a continuation of our labor for Christ here on earth. Or, possibly one of the many fascinating jobs involved with running a universe.

Whatever it is, it will be a matter of self-delight and will involve work that fits one's tastes and abilities.

Administration

We shall reign with Christ[78] over earth and over all that dwells under God's heaven. According to our faithfulness in life, we shall be given authority over the cities of the world[79] during and after the millennium. The judgment of angels shall be our responsibility[80] as well as the judgment of the Twelve Tribes of Israel.[81]

Just what form that authority will take is not stated, but it will be perfectly suited to our abilities. We will be the undisputed, unthreatened rulers of something, who will lovingly understand and administer the subjects committed to our trust.

Fellowship

To relax around the table with Abraham, Isaac and Jacob,[82] to gather with Jesus for the marriage supper of the Lamb,[83] along with myriads of angels, innumerable members of the church of the first-born and with God,[84] suggests limitless opportunities for fellowship. And we'll have lots to talk about. In our new non-threatened state, we will be able to focus all of our attention, not on self, but on others, and spend all the time necessary getting to know them.

Learning

We will not know everything in Heaven, for only God is ominiscient, but will have a limitless capacity to learn. In the Fall, a curtain was lowered, which has caused us to "see through a glass darkly," but in Heaven that curtain will be lifted, and "I shall know, even also as I am known."[85] One of the great joys of Heaven will be that of taking all the time necessary to unravel all the mysteries about God, about man, and about the universe.

Rest

One characteristic of Hell is that those who reject Christ will never rest from their torment, day or night.[86] In sharp contrast, Heaven promises rest from all of our labor,[87] and from all of our trials.[88]

A glorified spiritual body will know nothing of fatigue or exhaustion, so the continuing rest that God promises will not be a rest from work but a rest from want.

No person thinks himself rich until he has all he wants. In Heaven, for the first time, we will be fully satisfied.[89]

How Will We Get There?

Elijah was taken up in a chariot of fire in a whirlwind,[90] Enoch simply disappeared.[91] Jesus was taken up in a cloud.[92] We will be caught up.[93]

At the time of our bodily resurrection or at the Rapture, whichever comes first, the composition of our body will be changed from natural to spiritual, from perishable to imperishable, from dishonor to glory, and from weak to powerful. It will no longer be like its prototype, Adam, but will now be fashioned after the image of the heavenly body of Jesus Christ.[94]

The composition of our new body will enable us to be lifted out of and through all the impediments of earth, space, and time, even through Satan's domain in the atmosphere and into our eternal home.

What's All This Talk about Rewards?

Rewards are of very little interest to many of us—unless—everyone else is getting one and I am not. God will never be any man's debtor. He always pays for services rendered.

Salvation is a gift, but rewards or prizes are earned through the quality of our service.[95] These take on the form of crowns or wreaths[96] much like those awarded in the earthly Olympic games. Jesus also speaks of dividends,[97] and Heaven itself is a reward. Whatever form these rewards will take, they will constitute divine recognition for human effort—the highest praise that can be given to man.

A young son was dying. Both father and mother watched day after day as the life slowly ebbed from his body.

The father sat beside the boy's bed one evening, took his hand, and said, "Son, do you know you are dying?"

"No . . . am I?"

"Yes, my son, you are dying."

"Will I live the day out?"

"No, you may die at any moment."

He looked up at his father and said, "Well, I will be with Jesus then, won't I?"

"Yes, my son, you will be with Jesus," the father answered. With that, the father turned away to conceal his tears.

"Father, you don't need to cry. When I get to Heaven I will go straight to Jesus to tell Him that ever since I can remember, you have tried to lead me to Him."

For faithfulness like that, it will seem so appropriate and so fulfilling to hear Jesus say, "Well done, good and faithful servant."[98]

Will I Really Enjoy Spending All That Time with Jesus?

Unholiness always feels uncomfortable in the presence of holiness. Were it not for the fact that we will have been changed,[99] I'm afraid that we might feel that same discomfort with Jesus. Scripture tells us, however, that we will not only see Him, we will be *like* Him.[100] Because all our interests will be similar, we will be able to relax in His presence and supremely enjoy Him.

Most of us enjoy being with someone who recognizes our personhood, who values our self-worth and sees us as truly valuable. Someone who accepts us fully and loves us in spite of our past. Few of us know such a person other than Jesus, One who delights in playing the role of Father to earth's prodigal sons and in receiving us without reluctance.[101]

What's So
Wonderful about Heaven?

Different things to different people. To the poor it may be wealth, to the sick it may be health. To the imprisoned it may be freedom. To the persecuted it may be relief. To the lonely it may be people. To the dying it may be life. To all of us it's Jesus and the privilege of studying Him in His own environment and watching Him control His universe.

To most of us—imperfect ones—it's the promise of perfection. "We shall be like Him."[102] "We shall bear the image of the heavenly."[103]

The frustration of failure, the agony of guilt, and the reality of sin will no longer exist. We will—finally—be free from sin's penalty, sin's power, and sin's presence.

But I'm Afraid of Dying

Who isn't? Death is the last enemy and a potent one. It has us all frightened to the point of spending billions of dollars annually in a vain attempt to avoid it. Even Jesus resisted it in His last hours.

Knowing what we do about life and Heaven, most of us do not fear death nearly as much as *dying*. It is dying that hurts and humiliates and separates and destroys.

It's dying that makes it hard for us to talk about Heaven. Nevertheless, our loving God has promised grace for every circumstance[104] in life, which means God has promised dying grace—and that's just what we will have.

The story is told of a little girl who, one dark night, was walking through the woods to the river with her father. Far away the lights twinkled on a distant shore.

The child was weary, sleepy, and frightened.

Her father held her close as they watched the ferry drawing closer and closer until finally they were safe in the boat.

After leaving the land, she again became frightened and said, "Daddy, I can't see the shore. It's very dark, Daddy, I'm afraid."

"Don't be frightened, dear," said her father.

"The pilot knows the way—we'll soon be there."

It wasn't long before they were at home and in the arms of loved ones.

Some time later this same little girl was dying, and she stood beside another river far deeper and darker.

She awakened for a while and looked up to her mother and father standing beside her bed and said, "Daddy, I have come to the river again, and the ferryman is waiting to take me across."

"Does it seem as dark and as cold as when you went over the other river?" her daddy asked.

"Oh no—there is no darkness here. The river sparkles like diamonds and the boat is bright with light. I am not afraid of the ferryman."

"Can you see over the river?" he asked.

"Oh yes, there is a great and beautiful city there all filled with light, and I hear the angels singing," she said.

"Do you see anyone on the other side?" he asked.

"Yes, yes, I see the most beautiful form, and He's calling to me. Oh, ferryman, hurry, hurry, it's Jesus, my beautiful Jesus. Oh, I'm coming, Jesus." And she crossed over the river of death made smooth and beautiful by the grace of God.

How Do I Get Into Heaven?

Heaven's doors are always open, and anyone is invited to enter in. Jesus, the way to Heaven, is not willing that one person should perish, but that everyone may experience eternal life.

The sobering news about Heaven, however, is that many of the "roads to Heaven" people take will never get them there. Good works won't. Neither will good intentions, meditation, mystical enlightenment, or social service.

Jesus said, "I am the door; if anyone enters through me, he shall be saved. . . ."[105]

To enter that "Door" means simply to admit to the fact of sin in your life, acknowledge your helplessness apart from Christ, and finally ask Him to forgive you, inviting Him to take control of your life.

Stepping through that door begins the journey toward your eternal home. For some, the journey may be long. For others, very, very short. Perhaps only a few steps.

But the best part of all is this: The One who waits at the end is also the One who walks by your side.[106]

And walking with Jesus is a taste of Heaven every day!

[1] Acts 7:56
[2] Acts 14:19
[3] 2 Corinthians 12:3, 4
[4] 2 Corinthians 12:4
[5] 1 Corinthians 2:9
[6] Ephesians 4:8-10
[7] Acts 1:11
[8] 1 Thessalonians 4:16
[9] 1 Thessalonians 4:17
[10] Psalm 53:2
[11] Psalm 121:1
[12] Revelation 4:1
[13] Revelation 21:2
[14] Jeremiah 23:24
[15] Revelation 21:16
[16] Hebrews 11:8-10
[17] John 14:2
[18] Revelation 21:16
[19] Revelation 22:14
[20] John 14:2
[21] Revelation 4:2
[22] Revelation 4:3
[23] Revelation 4:3
[24] Revelation 4:4
[25] Revelation 4:4
[26] Revelation 4:5
[27] Revelation 4:5
[28] Revelation 4:7
[29] Revelation 5:6
[30] Revelation 5:8-9
[31] Revelation 5:13
[32] Revelation 5:12
[33] Hebrews 11:10
[34] Revelation 21:2
[35] Revelation 21:2
[36] Revelation 21:2
[37] Revelation 21:3
[38] Revelation 21:11
[39] Revelation 21:16
[40] Revelation 21:12, 14
[41] Revelation 21:23
[42] Revelation 21:23
[43] Revelation 21:25
[44] Revelation 21:27
[45] Revelation 22:1
[46] Revelation 22:2
[47] 1 Peter 1:4
[48] Hebrews 11:9
[49] Revelation 21:21
[50] Revelation 21:4
[51] Revelation 21:22
[52] Philippians 1:23
[53] John 3:16
[54] Revelation 21:13
[55] 1 Corinthians 13:12
[56] Matthew 8:11
[57] Mark 9:1-5
[58] John 20:11-18
[59] Luke 24:13-16
[60] John 21:1-7
[61] Luke 20:33-36
[62] John 20:27
[63] 1 Corinthians 15:40-44
[64] John 20:26
[65] 1 Corinthians 15:53
[66] 2 Corinthians 5:8
[67] Luke 23:43
[68] Luke 23:46
[69] 1 Thessalonians 4:16-17
[70] 1 Samuel 28:16-19
[71] Luke 9:31
[72] Revelation 6:9-11
[73] Luke 16:20-24
[74] Philippians 1:23
[75] 1 Corinthians 2:9
[76] Revelation 7:9-12
[77] Revelation 22:3
[78] Revelation 22:5
[79] Luke 19:17-19
[80] 1 Corinthians 6:3
[81] Matthew 19:28
[82] Matthew 8:11
[83] Revelation 19:9
[84] Hebrews 12:22, 23
[85] 1 Corinthians 13:12
[86] Revelation 14:11
[87] Revelation 14:13
[88] Revelation 6:11
[89] Psalm 17:15
[90] 2 Kings 2:11
[91] Genesis 5:22-24
[92] Acts 1:9-11
[93] 1 Thessalonians 4:17
[94] 1 Corinthians 15:35-50
[95] 1 Corinthians 3:13
[96] 1 Corinthians 9:25
[97] Mark 10:29, 30
[98] Matthew 25:21 (KJV)
[99] 1 Corinthians 15:51
[100] 1 John 3:2, 3
[101] Luke 15:17-24
[102] 1 John 3:2
[103] 1 Corinthians 15:49
[104] 2 Corinthians 12:9
[105] John 10:9
[106] Hebrews 12:2; 13:5